NIGHT IS THIS ANYWAY

ROBIN REAGLER

LILY POETRY REVIEW BOOKS

Copyright © 2022 by Robin Reagler
Published by Lily Poetry Review Books
223 Winter Street
Whitman, MA 02382

https://lilypoetryreview.blog/

ISBN: 978-1-7375043-9-9

All rights reserved. Published in the United States by Lily Poetry Review Books. Library of Congress Control Number: 2022932028

Cover painting: *Burn,* by Rachel Hecker
Rachel Hecker is an artist living and working in Houston, Texas.

"In the morning there is meaning, in the evening there is feeling."
—Gertrude Stein, *Tender Buttons*

Table of Contents

1	Night Is This Anyway
2	Breaking Point
3	Neighbors
4	Queer Theory
5	Q
7	Bending Civil Twilight
8	The Siren
9	Prehistoria
10	Polaroids

15	Night Is This Anyway
16	Bibliophilia
17	Ouroboros
19	Solitary, Poor, Nasty, Brutish, and Short
20	The Dada Kit
21	Poem The
22	Crost Bridges

27	Menil
28	The Twelve Hats of Napoleon
30	Pop Poem Seventeen
32	Scat Sofa
33	My X
34	We Are the Enemy
35	The Quiet House
36	Steep Can Be Mortal
38	Air Ships
39	Lucky Burn
40	Migraine
41	I Don't Know What to Do About the Faithful
42	Vocation
43	Coming of Age

44 Plagiarize This
45 As I / As / I
47 Lullaby for Myself

51 I, Parent
52 Be Yourself
53 Lesbian Desire
54 After Marriage
55 The Family of Begin Again
57 Red Rhythms
58 We Always Read Red into It
59 Nothing Rattles the DJ
60 Psalm
61 The Natural World
62 Night Is This Anyway
63 Thank You

64 *Acknowledgments*

Night Is This Anyway

The beautiful human machine
that I admire diagonally has grown
these wings under limited starlight,
reeking of tenderness, resting
in a bed of leaves. My feelings
leak out into the damp dark.
Walking over the tiniest of hills
I have no option except to listen,
listen and translate eucalyptus
in its innocence, bent over, grey
green, listing the reasons I fear
my love for you, knowing that
it could unravel the moonlight.
High-pitched sounds contain
random but true messages
about bones & loneliness.
In our fumbling 3 a.m. search
for the hotel leading to the room
where we would not sleep
until dawn, and it is in this way
that people begin to fly.

Breaking Point

If I wake up, I could be a dog

in a cool anime movie

a pit bull with wings

and eyes that blink so slowly

it makes you crazy. If you

wake up, you can make eggs

lots of different ways. Poach them, scramble,

be ambitious about eggs!

I might say, welcome to the new

order, dear wife. I could paint

a picture called Jane Doe.

You might remember something

that embarrasses you, but you keep

it to yourself. I would write down

a dozen questions that

have no actual answers. Maybe

we should refrain from kissing

at first. For fear of poison.

Neighbors

Some dogs bark at blind noise
in a hedge. Automatically the built-in
sprinkler systems stops. Garage doors
whine, then let their cars fly free. I
put my eye at a slot in the wooden
wall between our houses and peer
into your eye staring into mine.
A friendship quivers. As the sun
caves in, we are mirrors. A bullet
swims through suburban sky. You
catch it between your lips. I lose
my shadow in a maze of mending,
eyelids slowly closing, driveways
buckling in the rash sunshine,
clouds coming undone. Pleasure
is the penny on the swimming
pool floor. Dive deep.

Queer Theory

Between any two humans
there's a space, an unspoken,
unspeakable force field,
a presence that we
pretend is absence,
an electromagnetic
weather that emits
a faint violet glow.
Between you & me
no one says a word,
but Godzilla lumbers
up the movie theater
aisle, stalking the nature
of our relationship like a mail
carrier, making careless
jokes about matters of
the heart. I'm not
a sensitive person, but
I like to keep the monstrous
at bay; and hey, here
comes Godzilla, back
again, this time in our
bedroom, at a moment
when we did not welcome
the interruption, but
when he roars, we
roar along with him.

Q

The driver accelerates, as does the night.

I turn around
                and her words
slowly rise up, a swangling dream. We never
learn

              her name, just
call her Q. *This voyage
is not for you*, she warns.

But we are road tripping. Green
of the foreground bleeds
into grey of the distance. All I am
sure of is wanting you.

The lucky toothpick in my pocket
                          take it
as a sign that we shall remember a
rule or two here and there.

Because we care.

The kneaded and beaded body of
                        our future
may approach us with some unexpected promise.

One has hope although often out of habit.
Hope swims in the river of regard.

The barriers to love are everywhere,
like those large recreational vehicles
you are
afraid of. I am afraid also.

The sloping sky is a knife-worthy picture,
and pain,
                        but a moment away.

Bending Civil Twilight

These days last forever.
I wear long sleeves because
of the message tattooed
on my arms saying how it feels
to face the limitations of being
this way. As the sun vanishes,
stars tell their stories across
the retinal sky. Who is to blame
for the hell of secrecy? A thread
of lavender along the horizon
marks our transition into night,
a place where we feel safe.
Our story is our story. I touch
the throat of the elegant
planetary weather and this,
our two bodies flashing into one.
We are an everything.

The Siren

Heat radiates
from the
center of her
song. She
squeezes
sound out of
her first fears.
This music.
Alters the very air.
I sense her diving
cleanly into my
body, invading
arteries and
smoldering
backwards
through my
veins. She is all
that she is.
Already I am lost.

Prehistoria

The something that I was
supposed to be thinking about all
day long has not yet coalesced
into an identifiable image.
Like it or not, I feel my hope
sliding down a ravine into a tar
pit. Lying in my bed I hear
beeping noises below. I am
sinking into the earth like one
exhausted Apatosaurus.
Closing my eyes, I imagine
my bones emanating
an incandescent glow.
Good, I sing as I drift off to
sleep again, *good old x-ray.*

Polaroids

This is the hummingbird
hovering in slow-motion
above an oily puddle
in the red shadows
at the edge of night.

This is the street
that is so shy it quivers
like the needle of a compass
at high noon.

This is the gray factory
Smokestack that signs
its gray name again and again
on the pasture of sky
in a language nobody
pretends to understand.

This is the human body
floating downstream on its back
reflecting the sun back to itself.

In the kindergarten the long-armed
child is flapping, trying
to get some attention.

The only light
in this jagged landscape
is the moon's reflection
wriggling on the surface
of the river's mirror.

The big dog wags his mustache.

When the woman climbs
these stairs her eyes bulge out.

A stranger is wearing
your green hat. You
can't tell if it's him
or her or them.
You wonder.

Perhaps I should have
called this poem "How I Bit the Bullet"
or "A Handbook for Depression"
or "Burning for You."

The shadows all have wings.

Night Is This Anyway

I know that this time night

will betray me. Bright ashes

parachute down in squadrons.

I can forgive anyone except

myself. These thoughts don't stop.

I confuse sleep with death, open

and steaming. Neatly, I place my shoes

beside the trunk of a live oak tree.

Where is the blanket? What is courage

when the world wants to eject you

from its circle? Without meaning to I

question myself, wondering *what if*

they're right and *what if I wrong* and

the *ah* and the *oh* and the slipperiness

of sleep glides through my limbs

and when I ask for mercy I'm already ready.

Bibliophilia

A girl is reading a book.

It appears to be about herself.

The words hound her.

The images shove her

up against an ever-present

wall of shame. Tiny moths

shudder. The girl hovers

beneath the center

of a reddening dome

which is the theater

of the body. Her own body.

To fail is to fly, I would say to her.

And then, *welcome back, dear*

sister, to this excellent nightmare.

Ouroboros

After the echo

a sister uncurls.

I believe her to be saying

Fear the invisible.

There is no such garden

and yet broad

banana leaves redden

and gold blooms screech

into vertical. Seedlings spit

and wrestle.

Photosynthesis stalls

In the blonde afterlight,

and a smoldering emanates

from the wild.

I am the flagging

of the desire to self-preserve,

unrolling,

untolling.

And after the echo

there's the echo after the echo.

Solitary, Poor, Nasty, Brutish, and Short

after Thomas Hobbes

It's 3:47 a.m. and Godzilla is

counting backwards in

Japanese and a symphony

flies by someone is paying

me to say this if I forget

correctly you are my best bet

along the path of least resistance

I amble up to the stage

at the sound of my bird name

and smile so that I hide

my feelings even from myself

like that black box in the airplane

unless it crashes you don't have

to know what's inside you don't

know and don't want to know so

dust it off and it will be good

as new that machine she was

more than a sister to me.

The Dada Kit

Product Summary

Inside the old Samsonite: the recipe for plywood, hers and hers eyeballs, boredom, plastic replicas of small fossils, several types of glue, some mythological pandas, instant breakfast, simple surgery, half-poison, a compromise, all cascading down, down into the comical universe.

The Pitch

The Dada Rep lumbers into your yard swaggering through dew at 4 a.m. in the guise of an armadillo. Given only a few seconds to recognize its import, while it ambulates between damp blades of grass, you fidget. You feel some feelings. Twilight and mud. Elation and disgust. Quickly the image dissolves, leaving you wondering whether it ever happened.

Disclaimer

Used for masturbatory purposes only, the dada kit reveals the inner sensation of sensation. Whether the weather swallows or not, the dada kit remains the unacknowledged leader of the self-service hospitality industry.

Prophecy

The meaning (that there is no meaning) makes your tongue swell as you think about death and while listening to the frank music, your name is stripped of curlicues.

The Dada Rep

Alas! a dog beats me at a popular 80s arcade game! I should be mad, but it doesn't matter. Let's meet at 2 and bring Q with you and a suitcase full of sharpie markers.

Poem	The
Morning	Meaning
Waiting	Writing
See	Seen
In-Cat	Out-Dog
Like	Blind
Cleaver	Clever
Light	Alit
Destiny	Q
Soar	Grave
Am	Were
Was	Will be
Blessing	Bleeding
Song	Salt
Out-Cat	In-Dog
Calculator	Mouth
Evening	Feeling

Crost Bridges

In every background, a
rathery heat. One can never
predict what fire will allow
in a country of this type.
The rider of a mechanical

horse greets me saying,
*The edge is painted orange
and on the other side, a
graffiti question mark.*
I thank him with this

small package of knowledge.
In a mechanical fire
(sleep) I had a
mechanical dream speak
to me in a blur of bluish

motion. I awoke wet,
as though I'd just had sex.
Outside, a cry like peacocks rang
in the still cold. What's in
that bag? your soul?

The things I say to fire,
I say. Whatever the wind
tells me to say. A fretful
message moves down a string.
Something big, just the sky. Just

a feather carried by air, a
message crosses to the other
side. The cockroachy ambitions
of the father (the father in
a book I know) caused him to

identify fast apparitions, moving
zigzags. In the race for parents,
there were no winners.
I speak as a lightweight
in the world of woe.

Menil

In the museum library she wears
eyeglasses, but they are just for show.
No, she will not be reading today. Only
writing. Beneath her page, ridges of the
wooden table rub through the paper
where she draws. Here is a psalm called
sunlight. Here is a psalm called glassy
sand. What is that sound? Grackles
playing in the pale grey rafters, a song
of greed, a wave of grace.

Outside, the sky. A true post-modern
blue that proves her point: birds flying
right side up, upside-down, no matter.
Because the dream of love is replaced
by the dream of falling in love. The sky
dreams of the solitary cloud. It is
almost April. The dream of turning
oneself over absolutely to someone
new bursts through. The dream of
flying. Of falling.

Forward motion will bring you
money when you stare at the sidewalks.
Once I found a twenty in shrubbery.
That is a true story. I walk a lot,
and the bungalows start to talk.
I am the always of walking, and you are
the destination, the pure, unremarkable
but beautiful half sun. I aim my poem
at you. Every poem is for you.

The Twelve Hats of Napoleon

In the painting the twelve hats look pretty much alike. Tricorns, they're called, and when studying them in their invisible grid, one inevitably thinks of his face.

An allegory about Napoleon: The parts of his face had always hated each other. Like wild stars in a burning sky, many-a-time they came dangerously close to colliding.

Nose, mouth, eyes and ears, hair and scalp--they were enemies to each other, and only I know why.

The mouth made the first move. It picked up and traveled south into the chin's territory while wind chimes tangled in a breeze.

Staring at the maps of foreign cities, he dreamed of love. Hat stuffed deep upon the mighty head. Imagine: Men dressed as women, women dressed as birds, birds eating, being eaten.

Bright colorful flags pop in the icy air.

Glory he had truly intended to share.

Then the left eye began to pitch and buck like a rowboat on a huge and moody sea. Pretty soon it became unmoored and drifted. Its gleam played moon to the entire landscape.

The nose had always been partial to extreme means, and it resorted to various so-called Acts of God--flood, eruption, and then avalanche.

All this happened in 1815.

When the shock of dark hair joined the rebellion, the great face knew the future must be feared.

In the end one is left with little more than the desperate search for symbols--hat hanging in air, hat encrusted with snow, hat as signature, hat eroding, hatlessness.

Face it: We live for the knife storm.

Pop Poem Seventeen

Sometimes when the sky has love in
it, you can actually taste it.

I went over to Jenny's to talk about
Sartre. We dyed our heads a shade of

night, then we drank to it. The first time
I took a train into the city, it was birdlike.

The oily surface of the night-streets
made me a true believer.

Today I feel older. Over
my head, a flock of feeling.

I met Q's friend
at St. Mark's one day.

He was an angel's angel.
We had some drinks at the aquarium lounge,

not talking really,
listening to strangers:

*They say the downtowner
had sex with Rex.*

We learned quarts of this.
I wish I could undo what happened.

I am fine but
I wasn't ready, was faking

the ready-position like
there it isn't!

—flotsam aboard the
river me.

Scat Sofa

Can't make it better
can't make it worse 'cause
the revolution throws a
pale shadow my X throws
glass bottles into the alley
late at night these words
dehydrate like the
moonlight and the theory
of everything has
completely ruined us the
tables turned the black box
was empty the melon
hollow as a gourd so carve
a manifesto into the trunk
of a dead tree and who
could have guessed when
where why they told us the
future, and we didn't listen
here in Dogtown

My X

The story is over. Even
as I speak, I disappear.

Looking into mirrors, the planets
see their own images and look out

at me, angry, afraid. In a grocery
store two boys mop the floor.

Nearby somebody smokes.
Control, control. This is not

an awful smell. It's almost
dark and in my mind, radiation

moves like a tiny pair of scissors
through the elegant bodies

but this, years ago. One goes on,
learning from mistakes.

No, says the voice
of our pain. The passion

of loneliness is like
a test. We watch the explosion

on television over and over
and say, without irony, it is

beautiful, so beautiful. Sucking all
color out of the earth, to suspend

little pieces of ourselves into one
churning, cohesive cloud.

and held by our watching,
the future is an easy one to love.

We Are the Enemy

I force my way   inside

                       an imaginary balloon

where a ghost is going   crazy

          so much   nothingness   so much

    suffering   the filtered light   makes it more invisible

than ever   there's barely   air   to breathe

a ragged moth   and its shadow   vibrates

I try to be   more soldierly   but wonder if I

deserved this   sentence   and was it worth it

no   you get what   you   pay for

The Quiet House

This is where you   unspeak

your ideas as they   fight

and burrow into   the white

limestone of the   mind

water drips   slowly

and the echo   echoes

in reverb   clouds

of mist roll through   you

and into a huge   looming

open cavity the air   temperature

drops another ten   degrees

in an instant you can   feel

an ocean of music your   skeleton

is reality   reality

is just another story   I catch

hold of the dangling   rope

and yank it   thinking

secretly as I can that   history

is a quiet   very quiet

kind of   ghost

Steep Can Be Mortal

Of Orpheus

1.

As predicted, two formed one,

a son. They gazed down upon him

with tenure, each one rebuking

this certain ruin. The waters pooled.

The boy bloomed, his power, invisible.

Due north of doubt, an atrium

filled up with colorful insects.

2.

Homesickness, at certain speeds,

becomes a form of genius. In the absence

of discourse, one may avoid doubt. But

the boy must face desire, and if the

fragrance swarms, it is simply

a matter of bodies drawn out

in the sand and lounged upon, even

if against time, against intellect,

against praise.

3.
Music was his brother.

4.

Underground, he could hear

everything. Springwater carved

signs into the limestone. He never

hid. Shadows drifted into mist,

prayer into awe into love.

Distances knew nothing.

Echoes echoed.

5.

Only through grief could he play such

songs. She, gliding a dozen paces

behind. He, feeling her presence in

every step. The air currents shift, go icy.

He turns around. She disappears.

Air Ships

Puebla, Mexico

I lie on my bed with the windows wide open. From the streets below, shouts of children shoot through the room, a levitating celebration. I've been reading blind Borges' *Atlas*. I stop reading to write; I stop writing to listen (taxis accelerate with a spray of sound); and then I am masturbating, raising my pelvis to an imagined mouth, a flower is melting, and somewhere in a sea far away from here, there is an otter floating on her back (wet fur catches sunlight in a certain way) and on her belly she balances an oyster that she eyes, then swallows.

Has silence always been female? In the secret Convent of Santa Monica in the nun's bedroom, the cube of time rings, the only sound. The narrow wooden bench on which she slept is adorned with instruments of torture--the leather scourge, the crown of thorns--each night she must have closed her eyes to weathery clouds of pain and purity, purity that any day could slip out the window like a lost god, spiraling into the sky. Luckily there were only a few slots for windows. Luckily she had never even seen the door that led outside. Draped in white muslin, I see her there, in the corner of her little ledge. Like a patient tiger, I kiss her wounds.

Lucky Burn

Cancer was cursing up a blue
streak. The teal-clad bosses came
running. There was no learning
curve, just the daily rattle of dice
followed by fever. In the lining of
our blight, I
                glimpsed an expiration date.

They let us see
all the X-rays, spiral
jetties of the interior interior.

She swaps her hope
for a pack of cigarettes. Not really.
But that's how it smelled.

Let us pray:

> *Dear Rebels,*
> *Forget my little name.*
> *Stay far away.*
> *We are currents of feeling.*
> *We preach enigmas right*
> *up to the edge of the inevitable.*

Migraine

The blind machinery of science

took over, galloping into the core

of a gold-colored oval that wasn't

really there. That's when St. Vincent's

linoleum floor invited me to take

a little nap. I felt illness fill my marrow,

but the hulking night attendant pointed

me out, said NO. He lifted me into the air

by the downy lapels of my parka. Headlines

flashed across the mind's movie screen:

skirmish in emergency room! All at once

I felt trapped in hot vomit, tied

down in bed tangles, urging myself

to escape on tentative legs. I thought

I was running only to discover myself

sitting still. [This came as a sad

surprise.] I sat in an air-free invisibility

just waiting to feel the pain rain down

its pale blue music until self-pity

overwhelmed me. Desensitized, I walked

out into sunrise, Seventh Avenue, NYC.

I Don't Know What to Do About the Faithful

Blessings are not for everyone.
As the opening opens, the sky opens
wider. The day breaks
shattering shiny things on the skin-faces
of the believers.

Down here, in the transcendent
village, the faithful walk around
with pockets full of ions.
They tell me, I just saw your look-alike
hanging out in the back alley

examining her reflection in a puddle.
They say, see what has happened while
you went away? They say, I saw it written
on the sycamore tree. Their breath-marks
float in zero air.

Up there, as a spaceship beelines for a momentary
window, a girl's body near the bottom of a swimming pool
struggles up, and on the air, the DJ
breathes as DJs do, silently,
in cylinders of breath.

Vocation

As my pain begins
to unravel like the
giant nothing and
nobody I want

to be, I pick up
my shadow. We pose for
a photograph in front of my school,

and wearily, sketchily plan
for the remainder of our
future which includes
rainmaking,

a career for which I am clearly
unprepared. Thus far I cannot even
conjure imitation thunder. The
unreasonable

features of my profession
smell small in the wake of
my childhood which has
been limited to random

winds and occasional
windows. Several times I was
nearly mugged. The faces of
rabbis made me

nervous so I avoid that
memory and begin to
dissolve into a liquid sound
emitted by my mouth

that is not love.

Coming of Age

Because the child who asked me
to talk about heaven had a reason.
Because when you blow up a balloon,
you breathe your secrets inside it, and tie
the knot fast. It's all about the never-tell.
Maybe I should have known. How many
times I've asked myself whenever I
remember him. Children can be the most
neglected of landscapes. Blake's night of
no moon: the boy so close nobody talks
about this. Nobody. At the moment when
the room dies. When some neighbor calls
the ambulance. In a world where
expressing anger is punished. Or plain
talk: how can anyone be trusted?

Plagiarize This

Flipping through the pages   of boring old Freud   a big

          decision   barked at me   cold planets

                    flew on broken   wings a tree

          turned to face   the light

green   turned   away   a crumpled

          scrap   landed   at my foot

          where I found this poem

                    that read, *you just type whatever I say.*

As I / As / I

Dear Red Airplane,

    This version calls for
an armadillo, those summers spent
    in Mississippi, in love with you.
With you. Like a tight burn
    scar to be walked across,
I've been watching you.

I wanted to touch your /voice
    swimming beneath the surface / spiny syllables / my
fear opening up the stare / saying, don't you
    do things just like me?

    Its dull shell molded with gravel / I think
about its inner side / and only a few tubes
for parts / arma.

Seconds at a time, saw you with your head
    bent back. Way back.

Cataclysmic *caw caw* / some wildish colors
of beast flinging the flight out of wide
    wings / shoulder birds, our eyes
to the ocean / buy me   one of those
    shirts daddy please please, so
I will remember / where are we now?

Sort of cunning sound of water and being sucked
    up by that, now, how to paint waves
on this canvas: now, stuck. I love you I love you I'm tired of this
all these women, this one woman, the way I watch you, I'm still
staring—   *how   to   paint   waves.*

Your names all separate / under
water, the sound / love / seeming like
     no no steeped in salt / s-s-s-s-s seawater
stings my teeth / bom-bom-bom-bom coming of
the shark, parting of your body with my /
please.

Today / far away / the dogs run the beaches
    punching the air with their mallet sounds,
charged by their special summer constellation,
so they do sense these distances *ourph-ourph-ahhhh-oooooo*
a straight shot they've punctured from here to their stars.

Complaining, this version calls for gravel.
    This version calls for my father, love.
    This version emitting its *no no*. It is / don't
you feel it / calling itself out.

Lullaby for Myself

No, I am always saying, there is no one
except the dream of someone, you, in fact,
as the rain plays, and pain taps on the rooftop.
No one is listening to the tumbleweed radio
show. In the kitchen, I am dancing alone.
My mind, bushwhacked by days of restless
desire, is kindled as I wait for sleep to punch me
hard in the teeth. I move through an evening
of routine, uneasy in the emptiness of where
I've arrived, living alone without my kids, rocking
in my rocking chair, confounded by the tiny
bites of time. If you think of me, even once
or twice, I hope you will send me a sign, smoky
and skyborn, close to the ozone, centuries
above the mud, beyond the madness of punctured
lungs, beyond the hundreds of apartments on a street
called Windswept, beyond the Southern Cross
pursed in the sky, because my loyalty to you blazes
there, in that spot, a simple flame, a violent
flight aimed at all that I am becoming.

I, Parent

Doubt is my identical twin.
Careening across H-town,
the color green is ripping out
patches of sky.

Twelve exits past twilight,
my daughters agree they're
brothers. They test the
waters with make-

believe egos. Some weeks I
am never there, and my
homesickness becomes a
form of genius.

My daughters say,
*Love has a simple
shape.* They
assure me: soon

we will rent a cloud for
the weekend and draw
meticulous pictures
of all kinds of cats.

Be Yourself

We have our theories about chaos, and chaos has its theories about us

Remember Underdog the humble

superhero who wore a power ring on one paw   with a little pill   inside and what a weird

message for kids, to pop a tablet for the courage needed to repel enemies

or Jonny Quest and his dog Bandit, their adventures on barren landscapes   blank

as a chalkboard on the first day of school and no women or girls

and this is where it begins   the imagination leans   into the images

and teaches us   who to   become   how to

inhabit a boy/girl personality that your mother will disapprove of

a certain swagger   a certain jacket   a style of hair

that transforms us mostly in   our own tomboy minds and here I am like a damn hero

ready ready ready or not

everything I like reminds me of sex

I woke up in the madhouse but   I think it was a dream.

Lesbian Desire

My old mouth, my new mouth

They both want to meet her

And although she might expel

Words filled with philosophy

There would be otherables

Of this I am quite sure

I am talking about an economy

Of erotic communication I am

Talking about an unforgiveable

Attraction, the double helix

Made up of women entwined

With bodies more naked each

Night I am talking more than should

The landscape is thrumming

I am music

Somebody has spilled sugar on

The sidewalk where a new day

Begins by lunching on sunrise

And I (he/she/they) dictate

A love letter to a woman

A beautiful woman who reads

Constantly who longs for love secretly

Who pretends not to know

I'm here

After Marriage

In flying, bats unfold,
opening themselves
to predators (hawks, owls)
in the grey-dark sky.
We might, together,
play a game of silence
if we dared a taste
of blindness. I
am bats tonight,
except instead
of flying I'm lying
here on the ground
like an object ejected
from one paradise
to another. Cloud cover
reflects my love back to me
through damp leaves,
and micro-mist susurrates
the air. Every breath I take
glitters secretly and then,
like kissing, disappears.

The Family of Begin Again

To you, I say yes.

Whether we bridge or ford,

seam or hem.

Yes, as rainwater floods the bayou's concrete walls and seeps into the city.

Yes, and still yes, as the characters in this story handle each other for the first

time. And yes, as the run-up contains both threads of moonlight and anger.

There is a strand of anger wire-live and tying

down my tongue. A strand of anger that can

only be quelled by dreams.

Who can explain the small stone in my

mouth? Who dreamed the stone, my

mother or me?

I meant to say characters. In that story.

Because these are the clothes we hide in.

We ache for invisibility, for the escape from our own bodies.

And yet. You. And yet. Me.

Just alive, just bravely alive and vibrating

with words spilling out that hold us in this

grid and never sleep and never cry.

Red Rhythms

Her mouth is in a good mood
thinking about a circus

The fire smiled at me

Time came and went
riding a blue bicycle

I fell asleep
and the immersion made me all shimmery

From a swamp hut
I counted cypress knees

some jazz men fired at me
with bright trombones someone
doused the pyramid of wood
with gasoline someone
struck the match

The burnt smell told me
you are paralyzed

She held my wrists
I couldn't move

fear making such a lovely bracelet

We Always Read Red into It
after Gertrude Stein

Again is not just once
or made of miracles
but with some embarrassment,
one swells with curiosity and asks,
concerning orgasms, the how of them.
Very likely a sign signaling loss
a bright coin that spits
a scat song rushing
through pain into the spiky
edge of bliss

We resign ourselves
to the music
in the muscular
and we always see sex in everything
supposing joy
supposing the sound of tides

and supposing sand, the body
searching for secret breath
and what lies inside, releasing a blast of power,

a beyondable spectrum of **yes.**

Nothing Rattles the DJ

On the dance floor we breathe in sync as music files into our lungs the pulse commandeering our body the all the one with all the other ones here we are heat we are flashing free of gender, cages, terms we are a game of feels we are blindness split into rhythm, neon dissected by beats, we are more than electric we are young, free, motherless, sweet as hell, grieving, sweltering just-born bodies queering validation, donning invisible haloes underneath planetary lights and music is the rope harness holding us onto the face of the sheer cliff

                                      language is the drug kissing is the muscularity hips hold the rhyme high above us is the DJ wearing the matador hat and smiling for the love and beauty of the bulls we mouth non-messages to one another there's nothing to say pleasure is a poem you are tulips on a winter morning we are in love with you and you and you (us loving the all of us) and the cylinder of sound swells into sun, blaze, brain beeping, constellations of lucky stars and until you say when it will never end never end never ever end

Psalm

Thunder rumbles.
Goodbye, electric light.
I will sit here alone, waiting.
Then the voice of the Lord tells me
Grab a flashlight
because darkness tranquilizes days and daisies.
Lightning splits the wall of air
and gravity grafts the halves
back into holiness. Ions glow badly.
I swallow, anticipating
the edge of endings.
In my pocket, fingers jingle the knot of keys.
Counting by memory, I trot downstairs.
Here I am.

The Natural World

The forest takes one green
gasp, then lures us forward
with its darkening sound.
The starling says amen,
and we accept the rain
tossed from the sky
because our love balances
on the garnet edge of light.

When we come together,
we are bright fish leaping
in air. In the body, meaning
our one body, reuniting, we
remain hovering at the level
of all living things, breathing in
melancholy and astonishment.

Night Is This Anyway

The dogs scratch their backs
upward against the boxwoods
Possums pace along fence tops
The dogs howl them to statues
Here in the absence of stars somehow
the stars stare down at me anyway
I breathe and count, breathe, count
and wait for my heart to quiet down
Owls are swaying
Cats, praying
And, Lord, here I am
gliding quietly through the
dark I know the way
through dead ends and long
unmowed fields of weeds
I walk for the walking
mile after mile of it
until the soles of my feet hum
and I've sewn up the edges of mind
so that when I come home
I can feel the surging song
of gratitude for my sleeping family
Room by room I
check on each child, each cat, dog,
And then, back to our bed
I find peace in your body
I find love and its reverb
like rusty bells in my chest
a love so ready and real
that it gave me this poem

Thank You

Night is a seemster. We float through it anyway. Despite distances.
Tomorrow I will return the flawed predictions about snow,
the faces, blank and blinking, the nosebleeds, the visions of deer,
the dancing. I will relinquish the steering wheel, the free packets
of sugar, the existential and the mysterious, candlelight and mud
puddles. Tomorrow I will remove the shellac, the lip-gloss, and laminate.
I will forgo the power of now and the unbroken circles. But in the perfect
moment, I will light a candle and the glassy blue flame will remind me of you.

Acknowledgments

The following poems are published in *Dear Red Airplane* (Seven Kitchens Press, 2011, 2018): AsI/As/I, I Don't Know What To Do About the Faithful, Air Ships, and Postcards to Myself.

These poems appeared in the following magazines or journals:

Ars Poetica
Crost Bridges

Bayou Review
Everybody's Autoerotic

Chiron Review
Red Rhythms

Cimarron Review
Pop Poem 17

CutBank
The Family of Begin Again
Lesbian Desire
Night Is This Anyway [The beautiful]

Encodings
Vocation

Gulf Coast
After Marriage
I Don't Know What to Do About the Faithful
Neighbors

Houston Chronicle
Queer Theory

How(ever)
As I / As / I

Lavender Review
Bending Civil Twilight

Maverick Magazine
Plagiarize This
We Are the Enemy

Ouroboros Journal
Ouroboros

Poet Lore
Breaking Point
Lullaby for Myself

Ploughshares
The Twelve Hats of Napoleon

Salt River Review
Air Ships

Sinister Wisdom
Nothing Rattles the DJ

Swank Writing
Scat Sofa

Texas Review
I, Parent
Menil

Thirteenth Moon
My X

VOLT
Q (originally published as "But the Sky")

About the Author

Pin Lim, Forrest Photography

Robin Reagler, winner of the Charlotte Mew Prize, selected by Natalie Diaz, and the UK's Best Book Award, writes poetry and essays. She is the author of Dear Red Airplane (Seven Kitchens, 2011, 2018), Teeth & Teeth (2018), and Into The The (2020). Her writing has been published in *Ploughshares, Copper Nickel, North American Review,* and other journals.

Reagler is passionate about the power of education. For 22 years she led Writers in the Schools, and in that time the organization engaged half a million young people in the joy of self-expression. Now she is an English professor at Houston Community College.

www.ingramcontent.com/pod-product-compliance
Lightning Source LLC
Chambersburg PA
CBHW020914080526
44589CB00011B/594